ALMANAC

PRINCETON SERIES OF CONTEMPORARY POETS

Paul Muldoon, *series editor*

For other titles in the Princeton Series of Contemporary Poets see page 82

ALMANAC

Poems

Austin Smith

PRINCETON UNIVERSITY PRESS
Princeton & Oxford

Requests for permission to reproduce material from this work should be sent to Permissions, Princeton University Press

Published by Princeton University Press, 41 William Street, Princeton, New Jersey 08540

In the United Kingdom: Princeton University Press, 6 Oxford Street, Woodstock, Oxfordshire OX20 1TW

press.princeton.edu

Jacket art: © Andrew Wyeth, *Spring*, 1978, tempera on panel. Courtesy of the Brandywine River Museum, anonymous gift, 1987.

ISBN 978-0-691-15918-8

ISBN (pbk.) 978-0-691-15919-5

Library of Congress Control Number: 2013938972

British Library Cataloging-in-Publication Data is available

This book has been composed in Adobe Garamond Pro

Printed on acid-free paper ∞

Printed in the United States of America

10 9 8 7 6 5 4 3 2 1

For my parents, Daniel and Cheryl Smith
and in memory of the farm they raised me on

Contents

Music is being played to the cows in the milking barn. Rules have been made and confirmed: only sacred music is to be played to the cows, not "classical" music. The music is to make the cows give more milk. The sacred music is to keep the brothers who work in the cow barn recollected. For sometime now sacred music has been played to the cows in the milking barn. They have not given more milk. The brothers have not been any more recollected than usual. I believe the cows will soon be hearing Beethoven. Then we shall have classical, perhaps worldly milk and the monastery will prosper. (Later: It was true. The hills resounded with Beethoven. The monastery has prospered. The brother mainly concerned with the music, however, departed.)

Thomas Merton, *Conjectures of a Guilty Bystander*

. . . some of you are thirty or thirty-one and hard beset and bound to someone in brotherhood, perhaps in art, and you may see that the brotherhood you know is of a kind really wider than you may have thought, binding others among the living and the dead.

Robert Fitzgerald, *James Agee: A Memoir*

ALMANAC

THE SILO

In the country there was nothing
to do some days but make ourselves
scared and nothing haunted us like the silo.

It was of gray concrete and girded round
with rusted cables, several of which had snapped,
hanging down like severed vines. For years

the silo had stood there swinging its shadow
round and round itself like a flail. In summer
grass blades silvered in its shade

and in winter we shivered in its shadow,
baling our white breath out of the holds
of our lungs. Some nights I'd rise and go

to the window to see it eclipsing stars:
I thought they were being stored in there,
bright as the eyes of captives. Some nights

I watched the moon himself rising right up
out of it and it was like catching your uncle
leaving a dark house and not knowing

what business he had there. We had to be
in a certain mood to even approach the silo,
much less climb the rebar rungs that clung

to its side, enclosed in a trachea of aluminum.
Those were rare days we brothers
took turns climbing to the top to see

grain our grandfather had harvested,
black and numerous now as teeth
in a mass grave. . . . But the real

reason we climbed the silo was to see *it*.
What it was was a great hook that hung
ten feet above the rotten grain like the *mechane*

that lifted a blood-stained wax effigy
of Caesar over the heads of the mourners
while Mark Antony spoke, spinning

the body around so the crowd could see
his twenty-three wounds and believe him
dead. One day one fall our father

decided to have the silo taken down
and all that grain finally fell to earth.
But for years the grass there struggled

to grow, the first to frost and the last
to thaw. The wind seemed to glance
off an invisible pillar the birds

circled around. And one morning
after a night of rain (the only thing
that would go in there), I found tracks

where deer had stepped gingerly
around that blighted ring like children
who know not to walk on graves.

QUEEN-ANNE'S LACE

Queen-Anne's lace grew in the ditches
along Winneshiek, material for a wedding
dress that will never be worn, but will hang
in a closet forever on thin shoulders of wire.

Every May, Olsondorf laid fresh gravel down
and I'd walk the road in search of fossils.
I believed them to be the bones of dinosaurs
and my mother said that was exactly what they were.

The girl who lived in the trailer down the road
would come over summer afternoons,
dig in the sandbox for a few hours and,
deficient, lick the salt blocks in the pasture.

I saw her for the first time in years last night,
walking down the paved road pregnant,
smiling to herself the way she would
when she was digging in the sandbox.

I could have pulled over and said hello,
but I didn't want to startle her.
She was walking down the road barefoot
over fossils that will never be found,

thinking what to name her child.

FORT-DA

Nights they'd leave they'd leave us
with a babysitter who spent the night
on the phone with her boyfriend,
the whole house haunted by her

virginity. Lying in bed, I'd watch
the walls, desperate to see them
awash with the ash-colored light
that would prove they were alive.

Often lights that weren't theirs
mauled the walls and passed on
into the bedrooms of other lives.
How comfortless these lights

were in their passing. Cruel world:
the laughter of the babysitter
running up the stairs and sliding down
the railing, the rush of another

car, then the phone wringing
its own neck. Was it the Sheriff?
Of course it wasn't: it was
him calling her back. Finally,

I would wake to the sound
of tires on gravel like the sound
of a man walking with bags
of ice tied to his feet, and lie

there listening for their footsteps
on the porch, my mother apologizing

for the lateness of the hour,
my father saying, "Good night."

In the morning I had to pretend
I hadn't assumed there'd been
an accident. I couldn't hug them
or show any unusual affection

towards them. I had to say "Good
morning" as if they were dead.

THISTLES

My father would wake early and calmly
go about the business of giving himself
cancer. Red, the color itself,
sloshing in the tank behind him,
he'd drive the fencerows all morning,
spraying thistles.
I've always loved thistles
for how they hold their beauty
apart from us,
their purple blossoms
more beautiful for being
pain's fountaining,
like the beauty of the pain of martyrs.
In this way also they are
like those rare creatures,
mountain lions, owls, you
never dream of seeing, much less
touching. Which is why
he had to kill them
from a distance, a spherical mist
hanging in the air, a tongueless
bell of poison. Because who scythes
anymore? I can still see my father
unmasked like an actor backstage,
breathing as deeply
as he ever breathed,
while behind him already they were
beginning to yellow
like old, old annals in a chest
of drawers no one opens anymore.

THE NIGHT MY MOTHER

found the lump under her breast
we tried to take our usual walk
up through the fields
but even the clover blossoms
transfiguring into white
butterflies angered me
she went to bed when it was still
light tired from worry
and my father and I we
sat on the porch drinking beer
in silence until a car started
gunning it up and down Winneshiek
I could tell by the way the bottle
popped off his lips my father
was getting ready to blow
my mother lying above us
in the white glow of bedrooms
at dusk feeling her breast
and this guy flooring it
up and over Colberg's hill
my father bolted for the truck
so fast I had to run to hop in it
before he took off bucking
down that gravel lane
we always drove so carefully
we chased this guy all the hell
over Stephenson County
the back of his head brutish
and cruel as other lives
can seem but couldn't quite
catch him and when he hit
the highway I was glad

for him because I'm certain
my father would've killed him
when we got home my mother
was standing on the porch
in her white nightgown
wondering where in the world
we'd been it turned out
the lump was only a deposit
of calcium something harmless
her body had made we laugh
about it now but never once
have we mentioned how
we disappeared for an hour
to chase a man whose face
we never saw while she lay alone
in bed like a young woman
moved hugely by a novel

HOW A CALF COMES INTO THE WORLD

In the middle of a midwinter night, a light
comes on in a farmhouse. Something in his dream
woke him and now his wife is awake and now
his son, who follows him out to the barn lit
by one mercury light. One look and he goes
off to wake some poor man (*his* wife, *his* kids),
leaving his son standing there, the calf's face
stretching the vagina like a mask,
gazing the opposite direction of its mother,
strangled by something her body made
to feed it and which now must be cut, the cow
bellaring and shitting into her calf's mouth.
His father comes back, takes a handful of straw
the boy bed the pen down with earlier that day
and cleans the manure away, reaches in
and clears the throat of fluid, reaches deeper
and says he feels the cord. When the vet arrives
he comes in with his sleeves rolled up, carrying
a pail of bright tools plunged in hot water.
The farmer tells his son to take down from
where they hang on the wall obstetrical chains
that have pulled countless calves into the world.
They're heavy and the boy has to drag them
across the straw-strewn floor. The vet talks
high school basketball as he cinches
the chains tight around the white forelegs,
just above the pinkish hooves, then steps back
to let father and son pull, not at all angry
it wasn't necessary to call him, knowing
what it must have looked like before.
And when the calf comes pouring out, landing
hard despite the straw, he knows to leave

as soon as he knows the calf will live
so a man can show his son
how to get a calf to stand and drink, then wash
the chain link by link, even as the barn
cats slink in, ravenous for the afterbirth.

LIGHTNING

I love my father in the storm-light with it green in the windows
   and in our eyes, the thunder lumbering over, the parlor radio hissing
    under the shy voice of the meteorologist. I still have calves to feed.
      I know they're hungry, but I can't walk out into that electric timber
       and let the lightning set its crown of white thorns upon my head.
        It happened to my grandfather once: he stepped out like an actor
         stepping onto the stage to say a soliloquy, rubber-booted, thank God,
          only to feel his hair lift like sea kelp, then the white shock and swell
           of it: came in singed and jaw-working, like a man who's seen something
            miraculous and now must change his life, his boots melted, the soles
             impressed with the shapes of grasses, the fuses blown out of his bones.

           And thus the genealogic fear of lightning, passed down from fathers
            to sons like lightning itself. So I don't go out now but remain with him,
          our faces lit by the halogen lamps of the weigh jars as the cows lighten
         gallon by gallon before going out to graze on grass they'll turn into milk
        while we sleep. How they can stand out in that treeless field and not
       be struck must be because the lightning doesn't thirst for their bones
      the way it thirsts for ours, who sit in pews Sundays praying to be regarded.
     I will let this storm pass over while the cows go out into the greenish air
    and the halved sky collides with itself, setting the warm milk trembling
   in the weigh jars, failing again to tell my father I love him even as he and I
stand together in the storm-light with it green in the windows and in our eyes.

AUTUMN'S VELOCITY

A spherical acre of the lower night is lit
and they drive in in droves, their faces sea-
green with radio, to watch the last rage
and violence of adolescence burn itself out
in the bodies of boys who, years from now,
having become their fathers, will come
watch their sons do the same, and on and on
like this forever. They shook upon this night
and town years before and descend upon it now,
driving down Main Street slow in the long
shadow of a defeat suffered decades ago,
remembering a late hit or somebody's spit.
Now they're meeting on this field in the bodies
of their sons to finally settle it. The sonless ones
either stay home listening on battered radios
or remain in the bleacher shadows, picking
a number for a son, rooting him on as if it is
their blood that purls in his body. But first
the band: some of them will never touch
their instruments again, but a few have begun
to become obsessed. They march in
militarily, the music angular, incantatory,
the drums booming like distant cannon,
the music the music of a field more ancient
and ragged than this one. The loudspeaker
speaks and the voice of the local mechanic
reaches into the oak grove where boys who don't
care who wins smoke. Beyond the egg of light
in which a violence is incubating and beyond
even the smoking boys is darkness, tools
of harvest left in fields taken two months before,
legendarily huge and elusive deer, and something

unnamable. Above the packed bleachers hovers
a firmament of breath and steam from hot chocolate.
Silver flasks are pulled from pockets and passed
around tight pockets of men, the history teacher
muttering, "For God's sake this is a school,"
but where there is violence there will be whiskey
and they take the shots hard like soldiers
about to have a limb sawn off. Indeed, watching
their sons play is like watching some part
of themselves breaking off and becoming winged.
Across the way even the visitor stands are full.
The other town is dead tonight: almost no
one walks down the dark and leaf-strewn streets.
The visiting team emerges first, their cleats
clicking on the asphalt like the hooves of a cavalry.
Their helmets glaring, they're savage looking
in their foreignness, though they're just boys
from the next town north trotting around a field.
Programs flutter out and the air becomes ordered
into names and numbers. This will be the last
autumn the senior's last name will find itself
in the strange mouths of another town,
his last chance to be interviewed for the paper,
to get free breakfast at the cafe for the hit
or catch he will or won't make tonight. Soon
he'll be one of the watchers too, clinging to
the chain link fence; older, he will stand
in the bleacher shadows, picking a kid
about his size and speed to breathe through.
Some are aware that soon all all this will be will be
a memory, especially those whose fathers drove
them hardest: for these, each second rings
with the knowledge they are nearing the end.
There are those who, no matter how good
they are, cannot wait for this last game to be over,
who would, if they could, be one of the boys
smoking in the oaks (who, hearing something
in the corn, have turned their backs to the game).

But now the home team appears, the crowd
stands as one and roars and it is clear it is time:
the game must be played. What took them
so long was the prayer, the boys kneeling
as if receiving absolution, and in a way they were,
though what sins they were being absolved of
it is difficult to say. Maybe it was the sin of being
sons at all. Tonight they have been asked to be
great for the sake of their fathers. If the bleachers
were empty they would play with the giddiness
of schoolboys. Instead, because their fathers are
watching, they approach the field solemnly,
despite the fact they're sprinting now. Deep
in their facemasks their faces are pale,
as if it's perfectly possible they could die.

THE BRINKMEIERS

Mike Brinkmeier has just lain down
and because he's a grain farmer lies
awake awhile thinking about what
grain farmers think about: grain.

And Judy Brinkmeier lies turned away
from him, also not asleep, thinking
how to mix watercolors to get
a shade like that of violets dying.

And Sarah Brinkmeier lies staring
up at the ceiling, thinking of the boy
her mother loves and her father
approves of, his corn silk hair.

And even though the newspaper
will report that when the grain
bin burst the Brinkmeiers were fast
asleep, suggesting they didn't suffer,

Sam Brinkmeier has just turned
the lamp on again to read
one last chapter in his book
about dinosaurs. It's one of those

big picture books. He has it
propped up against his knees,
a picture of a brontosaurus
spreading across both pages.

AERIAL PHOTOGRAPH, GLASSER FARM, 1972

The photographer drives away, leaving
Glasser sitting at his kitchen table
staring down at his farm. He is surprised
by how surprised he is to see the silo
exposed to the sky, the rotten grain
a new moon no one notices but him.
He believes he remembers the afternoon
the photograph was taken. Shaving,
he cut himself at the sound of the plane
and for a second was back in the war
before becoming an old man in a mirror again.
It must have been March because the fields
in the photograph are plowed furrows.
Through them the washed-out lane flows
like a creek conscripted in the commerce
of pesticide. He recognizes the darkness
through the threadbare roof of the haymow,
bales good for nothing now but bedding
down a younger man's steers. By the grass
at its mouth Glasser knows the root cellar
he and his father dug into the haymow hill
and where even now potatoes tap their canes
down the white roads of their blindness.
Down the chimney, the ashes of some past
winter's fires. The graves in the family plot
look like moondials from this height.
He can't tell which one is his wife's.
Looking down on the very house he sits in,
it strikes him like a hand that he is this land's
last lord. In order to remind him of this
a man had to spend a morning in the sky
and an afternoon in a dark room, then drive

for miles with this photograph lying
on the seat beside him to this farmhouse
one would assume was abandoned and knock
three times before an old man appeared
at the door to find a stranger holding his farm
in hands stained with silver. Of course
Glasser didn't hesitate to take two tattered bills
out of his wallet, for to refuse the photograph
would have been to refuse his life.
He had to buy back what had been taken
from him, despite the fact the photographer
was asking too much for something he had stolen.
Soon Glasser will have to find the strength
to stand up from the kitchen table and hang
the photograph, pounding the nail deep
into the wall, and at the third knock the hammer
makes Glasser will wake and wonder
who's at the door and what do they want?

DEAN

They found his father dead in the machine
shed, holding a monkey wrench in his hand
as if trying to adjust to the changes,
and sent two men down the road to tell Dean.

They found him under the mower
trying to unclog the hay his father
had warned him would be too wet to mow.

At first he thought it was the old man
kicking his boot-soles, come to bust his balls.

"Want to come up from under there a second, Dean?
We've got something hard to tell you."

"I can hear just as good down here."

"Your dad, he's dead.
Had a heart attack.
Jim found him."

"Sorry, Dean," Jim said.

"Dean?"

"I heard you."

"Now why don't you go on home?
Your ma's in that house all by herself."

"How's that any different
from how it's been all these years?"

It was really clogged and the wrench
he had in his hand wasn't the right size

to loosen the bolts but he pretended it fit,
knocking it around so it would sound
like he was making progress,
just so he could lie under there awhile,
his eyes closed,
in the cool, bruised hay.

COACH CHANCE

They were only boys but in the aperture of their need
they grew so they loomed in the door of the training room
like men who'd been wounded in war. One drill deep
into every practice they'd limp in, feigning injury,
though these were the more deeply injured boys
who, at home, were berated for kindness shown
to wounded birds, called faggot, had cigarettes put out
on their straw-colored arms. Coach Chance taped them
up slowly, winding the bandage round and round
the unsprained ankle, the painless wrist, whispering
so so so so the way one whispers to skittish horses
to calm them, telling them without glancing up
that they shouldn't practice, but should stay off it,
sit it out. How well he knew these boys who were
all the same boy, come to him fall after fall
in a different unwounded body, bearing the burden
of a different father's name. His sympathy was hidden,
guised as gauze and linen, but he healed them all the same.

THE MAN ACCUSED OF FUCKING HORSES

That first night he slept in the dark
attic in fear for his life and sure enough
woke to tires spinning out in slushy gravel,
the red glow of brake lights blushing
the walls, and lay listening to the yawn
of the screen door, then his name shouted
hoarsely, distorted a little, as if there was shame
in saying it, their boots in the house
loudening into breaking glass.
And when they left he knew that
would be it then, that they had done
all anyone in that county had the heart
to do. Everyone knew his punishment
wasn't a few broken windows,
nor the few times a year he would go out
to find FAG or HORSEFUCKER
spray-painted red across the side
of the barn (whitewashing it afterwards
he was simply turning to a fresh page).
They all knew his punishment was he
wouldn't be able to bear selling all that
tack and from time to time would find himself
taking the saddles out to scrub a shine
back in them, moving the brush in circles
the way his father had taught him, remembering
that night he'd felt so lonely, not lustful,
just lonely, and gone out and stood
on the gate and done it quick, saying
"Sorry" out loud in the quiet barn,
thinking to himself as he put himself away,
There are men like this in this world
and I am one of them.

THE BAIT SHOP

It was assumed they were brothers but they were not.
Once upon a time they'd been bootleggers and they did
time together in the same cell, ten years each, twenty
between them. For this reason it was assumed they were

brothers, but they were not. No one ever heard them speak.
Whether they spoke when no one was around was, of course,
impossible to know. Maybe they talked then in long fugues
of conversation. Maybe they told each other stories they knew

the other knew already. Or maybe they just sat there
in silence amidst the guns and poles, under the large-
mouth bass and trophy bucks, the elk and the brass
placard underneath it that read: *Shot Somewhere*

In The Wilds of Manitoba, Canada. June 16th, 1967.
When the door joshed its harness of bells they never
turned to see who it was but just stared into the timber
of poles thin as young alders until the boy gestured

at the fridge behind them, or, if it was his first summer,
asked where the nightcrawlers were. Then one of the brothers
would open the fridge and in the glow of it that was butter-
yellow and somehow warm the other would choose one

of the Styrofoam boxes, set it on the counter,
and lift off the lid to prove the writhing soil.
No boy dared say the dirt seemed a little dry,
having heard the rumor about the graveyard,

but knew to nod and hand the man the money
his mother had given him outside in the purring car
in which she still sits waiting for him, reading
a magazine about how to make herself beautiful.

MEMOIR OF MY IMAGINARY SISTER

Growing up in a world of men, she was tougher
than all of us combined. She never brushed her hair.
Some evenings our mother would come downstairs
with her brush, begging to brush it for her, for her
hair was beautiful, long and golden. When she was
younger our father called her Rapunzel but she grew
to despise the nickname. Most nights she'd say no
and watching my mother climb back up those stairs
with that brush that had been her mother's and her
mother's mother's was the saddest thing. My sister
loved horses more than people, spoke of Montana
as if it were the only place where there were horses.
She said in Montana after you die you become a horse,
that was your Heaven. We all just smiled, like when
a boy says he wants to be an astronaut. But she meant it
when she said she was moving there. The night before
she left she came downstairs and let our mother brush her
hair one last time. "Just like Rapunzel," our father said
under his breath, a mischievous look in his eye.
My sister allowed it. That night she and I stayed up long
after everyone had gone to bed, listening to the radio.
In the morning she was gone before anyone could say
goodbye. My parents went out West once to see her
but came back shaking their heads. She'd met a man
who called himself a cowboy and lived with him
on what he called a ranch where they kept what
he called two horses. She worked waiting tables
at a diner in town and he, he claimed, worked cattle.
To this day I haven't heard from her but I know
I had a sister once because I found my mother's
brush in a drawer last winter and saw matted there
hair the color of gold or of straw ready to bale.

NEON APOTHEOSIS

Friday nights the machinist ceases being
a machinist. Third shift drifts in, touches
fists with second shift, but the machinist
doesn't go to Durty Nelly's with his friends:
it's straight westward toward the gig,
through the green and apostolic corn,
something fervent about the fields,
as if an absolution were being performed
over them by something maimed and invisible.
The guitar is in its case like a coffin
maker taking a nap in a casket.
Four cigarettes pass passively through him
and he drives with his wrists, his hands
hanging like pheasants pinioned to a barn wall,
the radio on low, but within him the music
is already beginning to rise like nameless
white birds rising out of a demilitarized zone.
"You can't sing the blues in the sun" he sings,
and the sun leans its sledge against his forehead,
heads home. Now the land is a grave being
shoveled in. The bikers are out, flocks of birds
moving from body of water to body
of water. They pass him in pairs and he knows
by the time he gets there they'll already be
on third beers. The first thing the owner says
when he walks in is "You must be the music,"
and the machinist nods, though it wasn't
phrased like a question but as a command.
A few turn to see who Dave's hired
to try and move them tonight. Breathless
the bikers are in their black bodices,
the leather still hot from the day,

the heat having found a haven in what once
was flesh. A few plunge their stares into him
as if cooling red-hot tools in cold water.
He is cold water. The bar is full of white
people wearing black leather and in walks
a black man wearing a white shirt and even
though this is northwestern Illinois still
he knows he's going to have to earn it,
having played gigs further north only
to find himself singing to their black backs,
their skull-and-flame bandanas, swaying
in spite of themselves to his music.
You must be the music he whispers
through the major keys of his teeth.
The amp bestows the radiant snow of its static.
The light outside is desperate in its dying,
a broke man donating blood.
One of the waitresses, the nice one,
sets a burger and beer down on the amp
and says "You jess let me know
if you need enny-thin baby I know
Dave says the music only gets one burger
and two beers but you need enny-thin
you jess let me know awright baby?" He nods.
And now out of his long apprenticeship
to things forged in fire and years spent
with lathes, calipers, vices, chucks, drills,
shell mills, taps, countersinks, threading
tools he draws it all up out of his blood
into a single knife and with the first note
lops the night's ear clean off. A few toss
the pennies of their attention into him as if he is
a commissioned fountain finally finished
and someone says to no one in particular
"This guy isn't messing around." Another
flock, drunker, tougher, comes in on a warm
front of tobacco and the day everyone
had believed dead sees its last chance

and throws its lance clattering to the floor.
But with the closing of the door it disappears
and there's no denying it's night now
and the machinist is playing for real.
The music sounds like a quarry being flooded,
like glass swept under the oven, and now
he's biting notes off like they're paper
cartridges, spilling gunpowder everywhere.
The burger is cold flesh and the beer forgotten,
though his shirt is soaked through with sweat.
I'd say it's Hendrix but it's not: Hendrix
is dead and the machinist is nothing
if not alive. The whole bar has ceased
speaking and seems to drift towards him,
the orders slowing, Dave almost angry,
thinking *How dare he be this good.*
He's ruining the night's business, this man
holding a guitar like it's all he has,
and maybe it is. He's losing his life now:
it's ebbing out of him like blood. The women,
hard as they are, are beginning to fear for him.
And I think this, then, is what art is: this
machinist from Rockford, Illinois sweating
out a song in some godforsaken tavern for nothing
but a free meal and a few beers, but really
for that moment when, in the seething
silence between songs, he hears Dave say
"God damn this motherfucker can play."

BINGO

The night before the river won the bingo game
by rising up suddenly in its secondhand corduroy suit,
the arms of which were too short, to fill the square
of every acre, they sat playing bingo while the rain
lashed the windows like a jockey and the cars
swung the motion sickness of their fists at the dark
like drunk pugilists and the town grocer kept his store open
two hours later than usual to give the people a chance
to stock up for the big storm and if you'd been walking
down a street in that town that night you'd have noticed
all the living rooms were lit blue as jazz clubs with the radar of it
and the people in the bingo hall were talking about it
in the silence between coordinates and whoever won big
that night was forgotten. And when they walked out
they had to confront the brute fact of the flood, the way drunks
walking out of a bar are confronted with the fact of space,
the rain coming down now in long cords like the chords
of a church organ, the rumble of the river the sound
of a train coming at you through a tunnel before its light reaches you.
There were those who had left for the high country with what
they could carry, but they had packed in shame in the night
because of the myth that the river could feel fear
and that the worst floods were after the mass evacuations,
that later those people would return to find that the river
had taken over their houses like an occupying army,
that it had thumbed through the diaries of their daughters,
that it had drunk all the liquor and replaced it with sand,
that it had put on the women's clothes like a cross-dresser,
that it had climbed the stairs like an alcoholic father
only to find no one to beat up on in the attic,
that it had sat in the bathtub for four days in its own filth,
that it had also flooded the New England town depicted on the wallpaper,

that it had disinterred the graves of relatives its grandfather had killed,
that it had put on cowboy boots too small for its feet and danced
on the table to some banjo song of death that has never been sung
above water, that it had written itself into the will and named itself
the sole inheritor of everything, that it had put its head in the stove
and stabbed itself in the heart with several knives and swallowed forty
aspirin and hadn't died, that it had not died when it left
but simply wrote its number on the fridge in mud and went back
to bed to roll and pitch in fitful sleep for another twenty years.
But we were speaking of the night before the flood, the night
the man who won big in bingo walked across the street
and bought a round for the sandbaggers.

STEPHENSON COUNTY FAIR IN WARTIME

The man taking tickets fantasizes
he's taking souls, and maybe he is.
He takes mine, tears it in half
and hands me the lesser part.

The man running the Ferris wheel
has a tattoo of a spider spinning
a web on his arm: as he starts it
spinning yet again he imagines

himself a spider and the lovers
captured flies: he thinks of their blood
as something sweet and commingled.
The man who hands the kid

the BB gun assumes he'll hit one,
maybe two of the dented targets.
The stuffed animal he's trying to win
for the girl standing behind him

cost half as much as the kid pays
to play for it. But then, as if suddenly
realizing that the man is taking
advantage of his desire to take

the girl's virginity, the kid swings
the gun towards him slow and says,
softly, "Bang," and everyone
around them stops breathing,

and the Ferris wheel stops spinning,
and the couple at the very top
stop kissing, realizing suddenly
how alone they are, and far from earth.

NANCY AND DWAYNE, DANVILLE, VIRGINIA, 1970

Before the curator mentioned sex I hadn't seen her
bliss as sexual, and even after the curator said the word
I preferred to consider her bliss to be the bliss of saints
and artists at the moment of death. How else to describe
her face? Has sex ever felt like that, that eternal, I mean?
The boy has nothing to do with it: he's simply the grass-
clad figure she's exerted herself against. His body has
brought her to this final exhaustion in which such bliss
is possible: in this he is like a day of gardening, or cooking,
whatever it is that makes people sigh when they lie down.
And her hand resting so gently against his ear and neck,
near where his haircut is perfected, one of those remarkable
haircuts of boyhood it seems impossible for barbers to give
men: this is not affection for his body, only the bliss of having
been defeated. And it's quite possible she'll never know this
kind of bliss again, the sky will never be so bomberless,
the boy never so sweet. The next time he huddles over her
he may be a grown man with a bad haircut in the pain
of orgasm. They cannot rest forever. They must rise
against nightfall and as the dark ebbs its ignorant water
into everything, Nancy and Dwayne must hose blades
of grass off each other's bodies, shivering as if afraid.

ROMEO AND JULIET IN THE TOMB

After, in the darkness of the tomb,
after the fathers of the two families
had passed one another in the street
and exchanged condolences, after
but before the first ravages
of death undid their beauty, as when,
unthinking, a poor woman reaches back
and unties her apron, before anything
could be said to be over but after
the playwright had moved on
to his next play, after
the actors had gone
to the tavern still slightly not
themselves, still moving and speaking
in the ways of their characters,
after the actor who'd played him
and the actor who'd played her
had stood for a moment embarrassed
on the terrace outside the Globe
before the Globe burned, wondering
if what they felt was real love
or just a common and deep belief
in the power of becoming another,
after they decided they didn't know,
weren't sure, and went on walking
together without touching
through London, in no particular
direction, over the bridges
that vault the Thames like horses,
the real Romeo and the real Juliet,
lying finally in the peace
of the forgotten, turned towards

one another, and because
their god had left them nothing
to say, said nothing.

THE BATTLEFIELD

Before the armies came, before the men
drafted into them were even born,
the land began preparing itself, the way
a room will the night of a wedding,
the colors of the quilt deepening,
the windows slowly opening themselves
to starlight and wind. Years before,
the streams began burying themselves deeper.
Once a year a boulder volunteered
to roll down hill, splintering young trees:
afterwards the air smelled like lightning
though there'd been none. The wind blew
the big trees down one by one like candles.
These were left to season a winter or two
before being sawn up by a father and son
on either end of a crosscut saw, though
some years so many were blown down
they were left to rot, forgotten until the day
sharpshooters would come lay long guns
in the crooks of their branches.
Therefore, without knowing they were,
the farmers were helping prepare the field
of battle. They built barns right where
the wounded would need shelter, and when
the generals came they would find
the farmhouse a good headquarters,
centrally located, with a good chandelier
hanging over a good kitchen table,
just big enough to spread the battle maps
out over, and in that light they would look
beautiful, with a radiance in their eyes
that would make the orderlies say later

they knew which ones were going to die.
One farmer spent one whole summer
building a stone wall as if he knew
what its ultimate purpose was and that
he must take care to make it perfect.
He was going to build it one stone higher
but it had been a foul year and his cattle
were too starved to get out and anyway
it would mean carting more stones
up from the dry streambed, so he left
the wall a little short and went inside
where his only son sat at the kitchen table
whittling a gun halfheartedly. Years later
the armies came to that farm like moths
to the flame. Recognizing the familiar
landmarks of home, a young man fell
into line behind the wall and, trusting
his father's stonework, let half his heart,
that half with which he hadn't once
whittled a wooden gun,
rise up over the stones.

THE PIT

There is a pit in those woods
no one understands, too deep
for leaf- or snowfall to fill,
too far in the forest for trash.

I hear deer bed down there,
that hunters have seen sleep-
shapes in leaves or snow
and known they'll have no luck.

Generations grow up and make
myths, hunker low, squint
along crooked branches,
shout BANG and POW. Older,

a boy brings a girl there, lays
a blanket down. She says no.
Not knowing what else to say,
he talks of owls.

The boys become their fathers,
promise one day they'll take
a day off, drive up and fill
that goddamn pit in. But the day

comes when their only spade
is a playing card and they
know when they die the pit
will still be there.

They start making their peace with it.

THE MAN WHO POISONED ROBERT JOHNSON

walks home under willows, the moon
a paroxysm deep in their weepy heads.
He knows at the dance they're still trying
to extricate the bottle from Johnson's hand,
but his seized body is stubborn, a child
who won't go to bed. The other way
down the road here comes the guy
shot Lorca. He's got his head down
and it isn't shame. Glancing up
at the last moment, they wave.
It's too quiet for words and anyway
there's nothing to say. They're just
two men passing each other
on a dirt road in southern America
or southern Spain some August night
in 1936 or 1938, their hands swinging
bloodless and easy at their sides.

NAZI SOLDIER WITH A BOOK IN HIS PANTS

Put on book-burning duty, two youths
share a flask in the light of the fire.
When, every hour or so, a new load
is dumped off, they offer the flask
to a third soldier who, drunk, drives
so wildly books fall out of the bed.
The farmer's family is gone and no
one will come along and find them
lying facedown in the pasture.
Sometimes they flip through a book
by firelight before throwing it in.
It's like touching a woman's face
before you shoot her, the younger
one says. What? Nothing, he says
and picks up another. But while
his friend is pissing into the blaze,
he picks up one that feels different.
Thin as the spine of a seahorse.
What? his friend says, spinning
around and dribbling on himself.
Nothing, he says. You're drunk, says
the other. Maybe, he answers. He is
still holding the book. In the light
of the fire he can see it's a book
of letters by a poet he remembers
reading in school. The letters themselves
don't interest him, it's the feeling
of the book in his hands. Riffling
through it, he slams it shut the way
he has slammed certain doors in order
to put them between himself and what is
behind them. Aren't you going to

throw that one in? asks the other.
This one? he says. My friend, I hate this
one so much I'm going to take it back
to the barracks to burn it.
He shoves the book down his pants
and picks up an almanac.

SHARPENER OF KNIVES

When he is older the boy will remember
days the sharpener of knives
came, days like today: a gray day gray
as the whetstones the man lays out
on the white cloth he spreads
on the folding table with legs thin
as a newborn foal's. For their knives
have grown dull from cleaving potatoes,
chopping garlic, parsing parsley,
to the point where they've become
dangerous. The women press them
to their wrists in honor of their dead
wish to be actresses and draw nothing,
like the political cartoonist in the weeks
his son lies bedridden with polio. Older,
the boy will remember lying paralyzed
in his room of drawn curtains, listening
to the sound of stone on steel, a dry
rasping like the sound of the room-
sized breathing machines he has seen
while being wheeled past a hospital
door that isn't supposed to be open.
And when the man is done the knives
lie gleaming in the sun before being
carried in wrapped up in the cloth,
the silver dust of the filings snowing
into the grass. Years later, a father
himself, he will tell his son about
days the sharpener of knives
came and he lay paralyzed in bed
in the room above the room where
his father sat sharpening pencils

while downstairs his mother laid
the sharpened knives one by one
in the deep caskets of the drawer.

OVERLORD

I dreamt of a poolroom in a mansion
sometime after one of the great wars
that were supposed to be, each of them,
the last war. It was a small room,
just large enough for the pool table
and the mustachioed man leaning over it,
squinting down the length of the cue
the way one sights down the barrel
of a rifle in the company of friends
in peacetime. Someone had already
broken and I had the distinct feeling
he wasn't coming back, that now
this man was going to have to play the game
out alone. Except I was there. Except
he didn't seem to notice me, so intently
was he staring down the length
of the cue. Maybe it was I who
had broken. It doesn't matter. They were
spaced like spheres in an astronomy
diagram, the planets signified by color
rather than size, colors like those of old
maps of Europe. And that man seemed
a kind of god, poised to bash the spheres
against one another, to sink them all
in those pockets dark as the pocket
a man pulls his watch from to record
the time in a shaky hand in a little book.
But for some reason the man seemed
incapable of shooting: he just kept
gouging out the pale blue eye socket
of the chalk, gauging his shot. And
maybe out of boredom my attention

drifted to the tall windows suffering
cataracts of cobwebs as if it had been
years since anyone had dusted them,
then to the wallpaper with its pattern
like a young engineer scrawls along
the margins of notes he's quit taking
on the *metacentre*, then to a painting
on the wall, hung in a gilded frame,
of an iceberg, cerulean blue save
for a smudge of red paint along its base,
as if of whale blood, or dusk light.
And it seems to me remembering it
now the only way the painter could
have painted it with any accuracy is if
he'd been standing on the bow of a ship
that was just about to ram into it.
The mustachioed man had turned
away from the table and was looking
at it too, or maybe it would be better
to say we were both looking *through*
it because it had begun to seem more
like a window than a painting. And
indeed at first imperceptibly and then
faster and faster the iceberg grew
until the whole frame was filled
with that blue that was like the other-
worldly blue that sometimes powders
the fingers of lepidopterists when,
after a long day of netting, they finally
sit down to list what new species
they've gassed, and then the room
was listing, the mustachioed man
and I clutching at anything we could
hold onto, the chandelier swaying,
the spiders scurrying up their webs
like sailors into the rigging, the billiard
balls rolling around wildly before
disappearing, one by one, into the dark

pockets. And as the room began to fill
with cold seawater the color of green
glass, the mustachioed man seemed
to see me for the first time. Leaning there
on his cue in the rapidly rising water,
he looked proud, as if he'd sunk them all
with his eyes closed, with a single shot.

THE HOTEL

The radiator holds
its boiling water
like an accordion
holding its breath
in a ditch. The room
itself is simple,
the sort rented out
night by night
to the poor to make
more poor or to die in
but it is not night
nor is she poor. She
could have afforded
a nicer room and it is
day. Closing the blinds
the way someone
takes out a contact
that's been bothering
her, she lies down,
the only sounds
wrenches clunking
in the radiator
and a boy playing
piano in the lobby
like someone falling
down stairs. Clearly
he is unsupervised.
Clearly soon someone
will come grab him
by the wrist, shaking
him once the way one
shakes a thermometer.

Clearly it is a boy,
or a drunk man
who's never played
and wants only to feel
the cold ivory keys
the way a woman
will sometimes feel
the forehead
of a child she knows
is perfectly well.

THE EQUATION

He has solved it so many times before
he almost trusted the chalk to walk his hand
along the board and solve it for him,
but something suddenly went out in him,
not like a bulb, but like something he did
not know was capable of going out:
a moon, maybe. No, not a moon: a moon
thins before it goes out. More like a child
who goes out into a dark so suddenly
dark it makes him nauseous. It is as if
someone has gone out *from* him, onto
the green-black plain dusted with the snow
of the chalk. He stands there still, the class
hushed, expectant, the brightest ones
working the problem out in their notebooks
as if they could will him to finish it,

but the figures seem so strange to him now,
like cattle sheds on a plain, like buildings
built so some specific violence might be done
to voiceless things. The numbers are cattle
sheds while the erasures, still faintly visible,
are the foundations of vanished houses.
Someone coughs and the cough lodges
in his back like a dart in a bull's-eye

but cannot raise him from where he is
a boy again, walking out of a dark house
into the darker dark, sobbing. Then
he's freed even of that. The bell rings.

Forty men wearing blood-covered clothes
walk out to cold pickups in the dawn.

RESONANCE

The blackbirds are asleep in the belfries of the thistles.
The bells have been melted down into ore
and that ore poured into molds to make
little iron horses for the deaf.
And her little horse gallops valiantly on the sill.
And her mother folding linens grits her teeth.
When she is done playing the horse stands in perfect stillness.
Her mother takes it and wraps it in linen.
Later her father walks violently into the meadow
carrying the bundle like an unwanted child
and buries it in the earth.
The birds he scares into the air resettle.
The thistles sway like poor people moved by music.
The girl looks for her horse for a few days,
then gives up and sits for hours
looking out the window at the meadow.
She pretends her hands are horses in love
and runs them along the sill, the four fingers
of their legs, the blind thumb of their heads.
One day she pulls the white linen off the black piano
and brings her hands down hard on the keys.
Something resonates. Her parents run into the room
wringing their hands, but they're too late.
She knows where her little horse is buried.

POSTCARDS TO ANDREW WYETH

I.

    A shadow pivoting
    on its weathervane.
    The egg box inside
    the mushroom basket.
    War medals, frying pans,
    crow feet. All sizes.

II.

    Lime banks, fingernails,
    an aluminum canoe.
    Dead mice in seed sacks.
    An empty tin cup
    watching the bathtub
    overflow.

III.

    Bricks on a millpond,
    scissors on nails.
    A river stone, longing.
    A bell rope, deranged.
    A child . . .
    A chair no one sits in.

IV.

    A pine chest
    beneath a basket
    of seashells.
    A kitten yawning
    at an old bull.
    The sheepdog and his answer.

V.

    The simplicity
    of a farmer's kitchen.
    A splinter of wood
    holds the door,
    butchering tools
    hang shadowless.

VI.

    Pheasant feathers
    in green jars, distorted.
    Milk and blood sausage.
    The colorless ocean
    and a barbwire fence
    in the same window.

VII.

    A stillborn calf.
    Tassels in the chinks.
    Distant thunder.
    The springhouse locked,
    the cider barrels empty.
    A man on his bed, his shoes on.

VIII.

    The woodshed leans.
    Geraniums offer petals.
    Hogs wander out,
    grunt at the sun.
    Beneath the mulberry,
    two fresh graves.

RECOLLECTION

This I remember: driving north in what
was elsewhere early spring, snow-covered
hills running away like horses incapable
of being born against a sky the color
of a toy soldier before he is painted,
the pines spaced evenly upon the whole
landscape and the sense that I was
seeing the world as it was before us
and will be after us, the utter silence
and vastness of it, its voluntary poverty
beneath the moon, and I vowed to
return there some day, but haven't yet
and have indeed forgotten exactly where
that place was, though I want to say
it was southern New York, or maybe
northern Pennsylvania, somewhere out
East, surely, though I don't know exactly
what month it was, what road, what life.

LETTER TO MY FATHER WRITTEN IN A BAR IN MITCHELL, SOUTH DAKOTA

When you were my age you passed through
these towns on the wheat harvest, drank
beer in this bar served by this bartender
who was a young woman then, and beautiful:
thirty years dragging the same cigarette
through her lungs like freight has ruined her
looks: thirty years feeling the same bottle
of beer sweating in her hand, she's not what
she was those nights you and Dale wore
your cowboy boots and hats and leaned
against this bar gashed with stars and drank
until the brown bottles looked like grain
silos on a horizon, her cigarette good enough
for a sunset. There are still a few tunes
in this jukebox you might have played,
purchased with the dimes your sweat became.
You blew it all on beer and Grateful
Dead songs, singing in the attics of your lungs
Driving that train, high on cocaine, Casey Jones
you better watch your speed, then stumbling
across the road to the motel where your boss
lay worrying about the futures of grain.
It was the first leg of harvest: the whole
summer lay ahead of you, all
of Kansas and Texas, all those miles
of asphalt and acres of wheat. Dale's
death was small then: it was a moon-
shaped disk of ice on some country road
in Missouri half a summer and an autumn
and half a winter away. How could either
of you have seen it? You slept in the same bed
shirtless in your blue jeans like brothers.

ON A GREYHOUND BUS IN AMERICA

There were only a handful of us left
by the time we reached Des Moines.
The guy who kicked my seat in anger
all night from Sacramento to Reno
got kicked off in Reno in a dark lot
outside a maximum security prison,
the driver yelling after him, "You got
more business being in there mister
than being on my bus!" waking the woman
with Tourette's, who screamed and swore
for what was left of the night, claiming
the man to her right was masturbating,
until a prissy middle-aged lady leaned
forward and said, "Will you *please*
be quiet?" and the whole bus shook
with laughter. By Iowa the old woman
sitting next to me, who'd had her luggage
misplaced in a transfer in Omaha,
had had enough. She whispered to me,
"Young man, I tell you, I don't like this
bus driver. I don't think he even likes
himself." An hour later she announced
to the entire bus: "When I get home
I'm gonna put a sign up in the yard says
DONE FOR THE DURATION!"
The driver yelled: "I've had enough
of that racket back there!" He thought
the woman with Tourette's was acting up.
She'd gotten off in silent awe in Omaha.

MISSION

I return to the Midwest as light
returns to a black hole, having
thought itself sufficiently disguised
as music. I've been called back
to describe the trembling light
the granaries can barely contain,
the blades of windmills still
as the petals of pressed flowers,
the horse no one has noticed
has died standing up, who will
not fall until the boy who loved her
points. Then, everything collapses:
the granaries explode and send
slivers of light deep into everything,
the windmills spin so fast
they take flight, and the impact
of the horse's fall is so great
she makes her own grave. Then
there is nothing left for me
to do but go up to the boy and gently
crumble the gun of his hand.

THE SCYTHE

In the Stephenson County Museum of Agriculture
antique tools hang so close to the walls they have
no shadows. There's no one guarding them so I
take down from the wall a two-handed scythe
to give it its shadow back. The shadow blurs the farther
from the wall I hold it until it is only a faint bruise
acquired in lovemaking. I'd like to steal this scythe
and give it to some young man who's ceased
believing in the power of his own hands. I want to
get the kid cooking fertilizer into methamphetamine
out of the dark cellar of an abandoned farmhouse
and teach him how to swing a scythe, but I don't know how
to swing one myself, and there are so many
on the verge of exploding how would I ever find him?

THE MUMMY IN THE FREEPORT ART MUSEUM

Amongst the masterpieces of the small-town
Picassos and Van Goghs and photographs
of the rural poor and busts of dead Greeks
or the molds of busts donated by the Art
Institute of Chicago to this dying
town's little museum, there was a mummy,
a real mummy, laid out in a dim-
lit room by himself. I used to go
to the museum just to visit him, a pharaoh
who, expecting an afterlife
of beautiful virgins and infinite food
and all the riches and jewels
he'd enjoyed in earthly life,
must have wondered how the hell
he'd ended up in Freeport, Illinois.
And I used to go alone into that room
and stand beside his sarcophagus and say,
"My friend, I've asked myself the same thing."

SIRENS

My cousin lives in Manhattan now. When I see him
Christmases in the dying town
we both escaped, he says he cannot fall asleep
in the quiet of Stephenson Street and that when
he finally does, it isn't long before the silence
wakes him and he lies there fearing the world
has ended. I don't believe the world ending
will sound like Freeport, Illinois, but nodding
I say nothing. His tie hangs like a pendulum
gone mysteriously still in a closed museum.
His office looks down, he is saying,
on Rockefeller Center. All December
the tree blazes, bedecked in the holiday roar
my cousin can't hear anymore, my cousin
for whom noise is silence and silence noise.
Now, in the room his mother keeps clean
between Christmases, he lies awake
the way I would if I were in Manhattan.

If any house is going to burn, let it burn tonight.
If anyone is going to wake to find they can't feel
their feet nor speak, let them wake paralyzed
tonight. Then at least let the house that burns
be foreclosed and empty and the stroke
that freezes be temporary. Some siren come
comfort my cousin tonight.

A SERIOUS HOUSE ON SERIOUS EARTH

Having gone off to school on opposite coasts,
brother and sister will come home to Michigan,
their flights like sleeves of a thin sweater
being folded, she from her room at Berkeley
with its Klimts, he from his room at Brown
with its Van Goghs, to this their childhood
home with its Paint-by-Numbers and black-
and-white photographs. At the table they'll
take turns struggling to answer the question,
"What do you think you might want to do?"
This year it will only be the immediate family
and the dining room table will feel much
too long, its tablecloth much too white
and smooth, the turkey too dead, the wine
too red, and when they bow their heads
to say grace, their shadows will smudge
the cloth with the rushed ash of thanks.
While he thanks the Lord for the meal
he'll twist his ring four times moonwise.
Then "Amen" and they'll eat: bite by bite
she'll feed her entire meal to Stanley,
who by then will be arthritic and nearly
blind, shrugging when her mother suggests
she's grown too thin. He'll drink too much,
turn red, begin talking about what it is
he really wants to be, an artist, whereupon
their mother will spit a glob of fat out
into her napkin, squeezing it between
her finger and thumb through the linen.
Their father will keep chewing his, his
veins jutting out of his temples huge
and blue as turnpikes, finally swallowing

it down with the help of a gulp of wine.
The next year there will only be three
left and a leaf missing from the table
as if in sympathy with the missing
leaves of autumn.

POEM FOR LES, HOMELESS

You were somehow yourself *and* the autumn
in your black coat smelling of ash and Salvation
Army stores, standing broken in our door, begging
my father to let you park your car in the barnyard

because your mother was dying in Freeport
Memorial Hospital. You were downright senescent,
standing there like a remorseful arsonist, singed
by several fires, your voice a chain of hyacinth

blossoms and salvaged moths, all your possessions
boxed up in the back of your blue station wagon
which fell so deeply asleep on the cot of our land
it never woke up again. After your mother died

you disappeared. We had to have your car towed
and stowed your boxes in the barn just in case
you ever came back. I found your Bible one day
of farm boy boredom. The list of family births

and deaths was written in pencil in your perfect
hand, your mother still alive according to the dash.
I carried the Bible the way a boy carries a turtle
and hid it in my desk under mundane books.

The passages that had moved you you had
underlined in faint graphite. Mostly you marked
the red words of Christ. I gave up on the Book
in the midst of a tedious list of names and begats.

Last summer, in Santa Maria del Popolo
in Rome, I saw you being crucified upside down
forever, fading in the photographers' flashes.
I wanted to look at you: after all, you were

looking at me, or towards me, at least,
and clearly I had only come all that way
to see you, but I couldn't tear my eyes away
from the filthy feet of the man groaning

to heave your cross upright, one heel blackened
like he had walked barefoot through a house
burned down to its foundation, kneeling
from time to time to pick nails out of the ash.

ELEGY FOR MISSING TEETH

The toothless roofer, his son
was killed by a drunk driver
the other night. I never
met his son, but I remember
the roofer, his truck lengthened
by ladders and the silhouette
of his body on the barn roof.
Even in the worst heat
he wore overalls.
Because he had no teeth,
his joy was a darkness.

This isn't an elegy for his son.
Nor is it one for his father,
the toothless roofer, who's
still alive, and will be alive
this summer working
on the failing roofs
of the barns of Stephenson
County in awesome heat.

It's an elegy for his teeth,
gone all those years ago.
Where are they now and why
has everything bright,
his son, his teeth, gone
before him into the dark
earth while he looks down on us
with nails between his lips?

DIRECTIONS FOR HOW TO USE CREST WHITENING STRIPS

The rust stains on my teeth are from years
I sucked water from the mouth of the faucet
in the downstairs farmhouse bathroom.

Last Christmas, my mother bought me a box
of Crest Whitening Strips. At night I'd lie
down and lay them across my front teeth

like bandages and read Frost. I was living
in my parents' barn, obsessed with what
"Directive" means. Perhaps I was looking too

deeply into those lines *Here are your waters
and your watering place. Drink and be whole
again beyond confusion.* Some nights I would

forget to take them off. To think now of how
all night my winter teeth were whitening
in my dark mouth . . . I should tell you that

they worked, though when I look at my teeth
in the mirror the rust is still there. But do I regret
those summer days I ran into the house,

some tick my mother would find weeks later
already beginning to drink itself swollen
from my soft, blood-shelled scalp, turning

my face sideways to fill my mouth
with that water that was always the same
cold no matter what time of year it was?

Of course I don't. I just smile and bear
the stains of whatever was distilled in that
limestone well. The farm sold, this rust

is the only thing I still carry from that place,
and I carry it literally by the skin
of my teeth.

THE TRENCHER

How it ended up on our farm no one
ever explained. It had come to rest
on that land and what it might mean
to us boys born to discover it
must not have crossed their minds.

It was as constant to me as any tree.
No, it was even more constant. A tree
moves out in rings but The Trencher
didn't move out in rings or in anything.
It didn't move at all, it just grazed

in the silo's shadow, its great claw
curl-flopped forward in the wind-sown rye
like the feet of barn pigeons we killed
for quarters. Days of a certain gray
we seemed particularly drawn to it.

It was the yellow of machines
of excavation, but where the paint
had peeled off in continent-shaped patches,
rust grew like lichen. When we climbed it,
our palms the softest things it knew

besides birds, it must have loved us,
and loved our little bodies that were,
combined, the weight of our father's.
One of us sat on the seat steering,
one worked the pedals, and one kneeled

at the controls, the dials beseeching
nothing through glass shattered
as if by sea pressure. That was me

kneeling. The oldest, I believed
the correct combination of buttons

pressed and levers pulled just might
wake it. Maybe our father had tried
to start it too when he was our age
before he forgot about it completely.
Invariably failing and walking away,

The Trencher seemed disappointed
in us, like the substitute bus driver
who drove me home once, an old
black man who said nothing
until we came to the end of the lane.

I'd been sitting in the back of the bus
because I was the last to be dropped off
and shy. Swaying up the swaying aisle,
I stood there waiting for him to open
the door and let me out. Instead

he asked me something about rabbits.
I think now he wanted to know
how the hunting in our woods was
and to ask me to ask my father
for permission to hunt them.

I had to ask him to repeat himself
three times before he said,
in the clearest voice, "Never mind."
I still remember his bloodshot eyes,
the way he shook his head, the feeling

I had that I had let him down. Maybe
that was the day they buried The Trencher.
The men of my family were digging
a pit into which they were going
to bury everything they didn't want

to see anymore. They'd torn the silo
down the year before, leaving

The Trencher trembling naked
in the naked sun, and now it was
The Trencher's turn. Its grave

was a little hill of grass I grew up
to have to mow. When I think back
on it now, I wonder what we boys
would have done had one day
The Trencher started all of a sudden,

rabbits darting out of the grass,
mice spilling from the engine,
swallows pouring from the muffler,
the claw lifting,
our father running towards us.

INSTRUCTIONS FOR HOW TO PUT
AN OLD HORSE DOWN

This is what you need to do:
wait for a morning
that takes forever to happen,
one of those mornings
when God seems nostalgic
for night and keeps
everything hidden
awhile in fog,
then wait until evening.

During the day between,
do as little as possible
and don't visit the horse:
you'll only lose heart.
She is suffering
and her time has come.

One thing you can do
is find a length of rope
hung in the shape
of a racetrack
in the barn:
you won't need it
but it's a good thing to have.

If you have kids, tell them
what's going to happen
sometime in the afternoon.
They'll understand.
If you wait to tell them
afterwards what you've done,
they'll never forgive you.

Go out at dusk, at that hour
when you usually walk
into the field with oats
in your pockets.
Let her eat them
out of your hand
until they're gone,
then lead her in.

Then lead her in.

THE KEY IN THE STONE

Grandma Mary kept an extra house key
in a false stone she kept hidden in a bed
of violets. I remember the evening
she showed it to us. Our parents were gone
to a wedding in Ohio. Waking that morning
in strange sheets, we lay listening
to her moving around the kitchen,
then came downstairs combing our hair
with our fingers to the set breakfast table.
Strict in every other way, she was catholic
about letting us use all the sugar we wanted.
We spent the day so shyly, playing with toys
our father had played with when he was a boy
while she sat on the porch and read. At dusk
she led us into the back yard to show us
the key in the stone. It looked light
as a loaf of bread despite her frail wrist.
She slid the little plastic door open
and the bright key spilled into her hand.
"If you ever need to get in the house.
If for whatever reason you find yourselves
locked out . . ." For a moment it seemed
she forgot we were there and why
she was holding that hollow stone,
remembering, maybe, one of those tools
her father, a doctor, would let her hold
on snow days in his office in Milwaukee:
a rubber hammer he told her to tap his knee
with so he could kick wildly and make her
laugh; the coin of a stethoscope he had
her press to her heart so she could know herself
a living thing; a wooden lung painted violet,

plucked out of the chest of the anatomy model
staring out the window with such immense
longing at the snow falling into the lake.

WAKE

At your wake which was your sleep I saw
your son my father place an envelope
of soil in the breast pocket of your coffin
coat and I want to give you something too
so you may rest in the company of things
you loved the way Egyptian pharaohs were
buried with what it was thought they'd need
in the afterlife and so with you Grandpa
I bury three hundred cubic acres of soil
with all that soil is its living and dead
seeds its cicadas asleep for seventeen
summers its earthworms and arrowheads
I bury with you trees you loved yes even those
still green with life I lay them beside you
root and branch young trees of twenty and old
trees of a hundred rings the Three Trees
and the tree the fire-colored foxes loved
to dig dens under fine you get to keep one
of the foxes too but only the smallest
and least likely to live the rest get to go
free into the woods oh why not all twenty
acres of woods and all the woods contain
the meadow in its nunlike heart the fascicles
of its birch bark the fjords of its oak leaves
its rabbits and raccoons its fawns and deer
stands your grandson hunted from the redwing
blackbirds barbwire and the three-sided shack
it can all go in with you the snow of winter
scat of summer owl pellets of autumn violets
of spring everything the fields themselves
the hay the rye the wheat the barley
and the corn of course both its green ears

in July and its stalks shattered like shinbones
in November light the November light
every month's light for that matter light
of warm and cool evenings and every
evening's and morning's birds all birds
even geese just passing over I will snatch
whole flocks down from air and bury them
with you Grandpa and yes of course
you may keep your tractors and gravity
wagons the granary and corn crib and haymow
I'll employ two tornados to tear them down
into boards and shingles and nails and yes
you get their darkness too their mice and chaff
even that screw you lost that day in 1952
you get back 1952 all of it every night
she lay latticed in moonlight every morning
and all its dew the laughter of your children
the bread you ate the ale you drank all things
that sustained you your work jeans work shirts
hammers pliers screwdrivers wrenches anvils
every cow you ever milked and the milk itself
I'll fill a thousand Mason jars to surround you
like lanterns so you can see there is plenty
of room for both farmhouses their physicality
and their emptiness their doors and doorknobs
table leaves light fixtures dishware all of it
anything you loved you'll need the hill
of coal you kept in the cellar the green light
of bad weather the salt that softened the water
the bare sole swaying bulb over the workbench
the tire swing and the tree you hung it from
the gifts you gave them Christmas mornings
the simple humble barely affordable gifts
you gave them you get those back too
all that you gave bruises advice hugs birth
charity a damn comes back to you this and nothing
else is the promise of Heaven your father
and mother you get them back too yes

even your mother who you barely knew
who died in childbirth you get her back too
you worked so hard you were so gentle
so kind you get everything you thought
you'd lost forever by dying we lose
nothing by dying we get it all back

Notes

"Fort-Da": The term *fort-da* was developed by Sigmund Freud. "Fort!" and "Da!" were phrases he overheard his grandson exclaiming while playing. "Fort" translates to "Gone" and "Da" to "There." Freud noticed that when his grandson's mother went away, the boy would make an object disappear, muttering "o-o-o-o," which Freud translated as being akin to "Fort." Then he would make it reappear, muttering, "Da." Freud interpreted this game as being the child's way of dealing with the absence of the mother.

"Nancy and Dwayne, Danville, Virginia, 1970": The title is the name of a photograph by Emmet Gowin, upon which the poem is based.

"Postcards to Andrew Wyeth": After the poem "Postcards to Gunter Eich" by Tom Andrews.

"A Serious House on Serious Earth": The title is a line from the poem "Church Going" by Philip Larkin.

"Poem for Les, Homeless": The painting referred to at the end of the poem is Caravaggio's *Crucifixion of St. Peter.*

Acknowledgments

I wish to thank the editors of the following journals in which some of these poems first appeared:

Asheville Poetry Review: "Bingo"
The Cortland Review: "Memoir of My Imaginary Sister"
Minotaur: "Autumn's Velocity"
The New Yorker: "The Hotel"
The Sewanee Review: "Stephenson County Fair in Wartime"
Spoon River Poetry Review: "Mission," "The Battlefield," "Romeo and Juliet in the Tomb," "Aerial Photograph, Glasser Farm, 1972"
The Yale Review: "Nancy and Dwayne, Danville, Virginia, 1970"
ZYZZYVA: "Recollection"
"Letter to My Father Written in a Bar in Mitchell, South Dakota" and "Wake" (previously published under the title "Will") originally appeared in *Off-Channel,* published by the Midwest Writing Center
"Postcards to Andrew Wyeth" originally appeared in a chapbook entitled *In the Silence of the Migrated Birds* (Parallel Press, 2008)
"Instructions for How to Put an Old Horse Down" originally appeared in a chapbook entitled *Instructions for How to Put an Old Horse Down* (Longhouse Press, 2010)

Also, the epigraphs in the front of the book are, respectively, by Thomas Merton, from *Conjectures of a Guilty Bystander,* courtesy of Random House, 1968; and by Robert Fitzgerald from *The Third Kind of Knowledge,* 1984, courtesy of New Directions Publishing Corp.

I wish to express my deepest thanks to:

My parents, Daniel and Cheryl Smith, for a lifetime of encouragement. A young poet couldn't ask for more supportive parents.

My brothers, Ryan and Levi.

My cousins, Colin and Alex.

My grandparents, Sheldon and Florene Miller and the late Robert and Mary Smith.

My friends, Chelsey Weber-Smith, Janaki Jagannath, William Wylie, Lee Johnson, Stephen Hitchcock, Garrett Davey, Brooks Johnson, Kai Carlson-Wee, Casey Thayer, Eric Raymond, Quill and Chaponica Chase, Dori Stone, Michael Mott, Kent Johnson, Dion Kempthorne, J.D. Whitney, D.A. Powell, Michael Wiegers, Joseph Bednarik, Jesse Nathan, Paul Guest, Bob Arnold, Martin Shaw, Anisse Gross, and all the rest of you. Let's have a pint soon.

Merwin the cat. Big ups.

My teachers, Gregory Orr, Alan Williamson, Pam Houston, Sydney Blair, Rita Dove, Debra Nystrom, Lisa Russ-Spaar, Elizabeth Tallent, Adam Johnson, Tobias Wolff, and John Casey.

The incomparable Michael Theune for all his friendship and support, and for suggesting *Almanac* as a title years ago.

My lanterns, James Agee, William Maxwell, Larry Levis, Nick Drake, Townes Van Zandt, Frank Stanford, Thomas James, and Thomas Merton.

Gary Snyder, Robert Bly, and W.S. Merwin for writing back.

Samantha Shea.

Everyone at Princeton University Press.

And Paul Muldoon for choosing this manuscript for the Princeton Series of Contemporary Poets.

Princeton Series of Contemporary Poets